LOOK AT
THE ROMANS

LOOK

at the Romans

PETER GREEN

Illustrated by SAM KIFF

HAMISH HAMILTON
LONDON

First published in Great Britain, 1963
by Hamish Hamilton Ltd.
90 Great Russell Street, London, W.C.1

© 1963 PETER GREEN

ILLUSTRATIONS © 1963 SAM KIFF

For

TIM, NICKY and SARAH

PRINTED IN GREAT BRITAIN
BY EBENEZER BAYLIS AND SON, LIMITED
THE TRINITY PRESS, WORCESTER, AND LONDON

CONTENTS

1

The Accidental Empire

ROME was once, seven or eight hundred years before Christ, a hill village near the mouth of the River Tiber. The country round about was called Latium, and the peasant tribesmen who lived there were known as Latini—which is why we still talk of their language as "Latin" rather than "Roman". Legend says that Rome was founded in 753 B.C. by Romulus. The historians are suspicious —they always are—but recent digging on

Romulus and Remus, the twin founders of Rome, were said to have been born to the war-god Mars and a Vestal Virgin called Silvia. They were thrown into the river in their cradle, with their mother (as a punishment for having broken her vows). The cradle was caught in a fig-tree's roots, and the children suckled by an obliging she-wolf (see above). This story is usually treated as a fairy-tale. Apart from the Mars bit (which Silvia probably made up) I can't see why. And what about Moses?

8

the site makes it look as though the legend may be true after all.

To the north of Rome, across the Tiber, lay the huge and powerful state of Etruria. For a century or two Rome was ruled by Etruscan kings, and did very well under them. The Etruscans liked city life and luxury. They ate off gold plate. Their

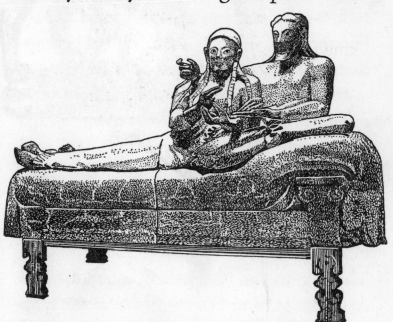

The Etruscans liked city life and luxury

kings made good laws for the common people. Afterwards the Romans threw out the Etruscans and said they were tyrants. They even pretended they'd made the good laws themselves. Ever afterwards, "king" was a rude word in Rome. When the Etruscans were gone the Romans were very poor for a time; so they said being rich was a bad thing—at least till *they* became rich in their turn: richer perhaps than any country till our own time.

To begin with, though, their little republic could hardly hold its own. Savage Gauls poured down over the Alps and nearly captured the Capitol, the high rocky citadel of Rome. (Some people say they *did* capture it, but the Romans keep quiet about so scandalous an episode.) There were all the other tribes up and down Italy. You can see them on the map on p. 11. There were Umbrians and

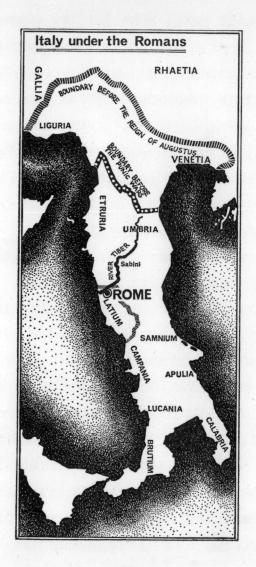

Italy under the Romans

GALLIA

RHAETIA

BOUNDARY BEFORE THE REIGN OF AUGUSTUS

LIGURIA

VENETIA

BOUNDARY BEFORE THE PUNIC WARS

ETRURIA

UMBRIA

TIBER RIVER

Sabini

ROME

LATIUM

SAMNIUM

CAMPANIA

APULIA

LUCANIA

CALABRIA

BRUTIUM

Sabines to the north, and Samnites and wild Lucanians in the south. These tribes began by fighting Rome, then became her allies. Later still their lands and people passed completely under Rome's central control. There was a terrifying invasion by a Greek king called Pyrrhus, who brought elephants with him.

All the time the Romans were fighting these enemies they were having quarrels among themselves, too. The Romans were all peasant-farmers, but some of them had held big estates in the same family for centuries. This made them aristocrats. These blue-blooded Romans traced their ancestry back to Romulus, rather like people nowadays who say they came over with William the Conqueror. These aristocrats, or "patricians", said they ought to rule everyone else. The common people, or "plebeians", said they should be allowed to stand for election too, just to make things fair.

In the end they worked out a system by which no one held office for more than a year at a time. This was horribly inefficient: a general, for instance, might have to hand over his command in the middle of a campaign. It didn't stop bribery and corruption either, though it looked democratic. They had a Senate, which was rather like our Parliament, and various special posts. The most senior was that of Consul. There were always two consuls, and in theory one of them could use a veto on the other. Sometimes he did, and the result was that the government came to a complete halt.

The Consuls were also joint commanders-in-chief of the army (I'll have more to say about this later) and responsible for various odd jobs like conducting official sacrifices, and taking omens* on special occasions to make sure the Gods were favourable. There was no such thing as a civil service till the time of the Emperor Claudius, in the first century A.D., and it wasn't very good then. The Romans believed any educated person could rule the country, and they were probably right. By the time you were a Consul you had run through a lot of smaller jobs first, including compulsory military service, so you had some idea of what was what.

To make things even more democratic, magistrates, Senate, *and* the People's Assemblies could all make laws—something the Romans were naturally good at.

---

* This was rather like reading cards or tealeaves, but messier. The Consul had to look at the spots on a sacrificed calf's liver and entrails, or watch the way the sacred chickens pecked. Professional omen-spotters were called *augurs*. The Etruscans began it all.

(We still use their laws as the basis for our own today.) They took the Italian tribes into half-citizenship, as they could well afford to do: something like ten thousand square miles of the Italians' good farming and grazing land had come under Roman control. The Romans were no longer villagers, though they were still peasants: they had the beginnings of an empire on their hands.

What really set Rome on the high road to success, though, was a long, costly, and almost fatal war. In North Africa lay the wealthy city of Carthage. Carthaginian traders and merchants ranged all round the Mediterranean; one of them, Hanno, may even have got as far south as the Cape of Good Hope. In 260 B.C. the Carthaginians held the west half of the island of Sicily, while the Greeks held the rest. Sicily produced a lot of Rome's corn, and the

Romans were afraid of Carthaginian ships controlling the straits between Sicily and Italy—what today we call the Straits of Messina. So they went to war with Carthage. The Roman name for the Carthaginians is *Poeni*, or Phoenicians. That is why historians call these the "Punic" Wars.

There were three Punic Wars, and between them they lasted for sixty years. The great Carthaginian general Hannibal fought Rome in the second of them, bringing his elephants over the Alps from Spain. But in the end he was beaten, and Carthage was destroyed. Rome took over Carthage's trade. She found herself, too, with land that she didn't want to make part of the homeland on an equal footing, but felt she had to rule. So Sicily and Sardinia, Corsica and North Africa became the first provinces of the Roman Empire, ruled over by a governor. They didn't know it was an empire yet, though. No one ever does, when they begin.

After these wars Rome began to expand faster and faster. The Romans kept taking over fresh countries to stop them being a nuisance, or in case someone else got hold of them, or because they had rich supplies of timber or iron ore or gold. They moved into Spain, and Greece, and Macedonia, and the strip which today we call Yugo-slavia. They got control of Asia Minor (Turkey) and Syria, and Egypt, and Morocco and Greece. The more places they conquered, the more slaves and money and food and ships and jewellery and riches of all sort they acquired—generally without paying for them. They put heavy taxes on the provinces, too. Later they made good laws for them, but by then a fair share of the loot had trickled back to Rome.

LR—B

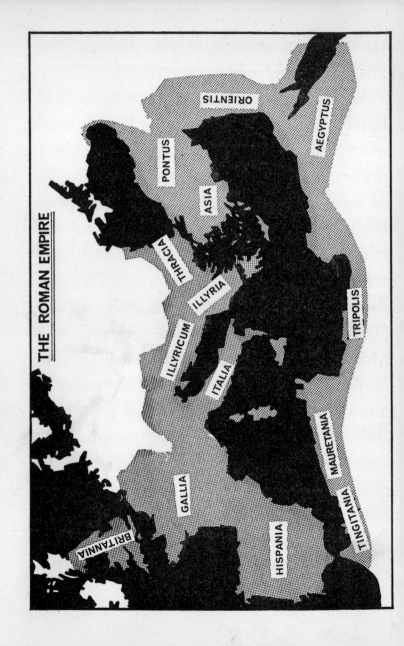

THE ROMAN EMPIRE

BRITANNIA
GALLIA
HISPANIA
TINGITANIA
MAURETANIA
TRIPOLIS
ITALIA
ILLYRICUM
ILLYRIA
THRACIA
ASIA
PONTUS
ORIENTIS
AEGYPTUS

In the first century B.C. the old quarrels between aristocrats and plebeians flared up again. A "popular" party was formed against the conservative aristocrats—the "optimates" or "best people", as they called themselves. Civil war broke out. An aristocrat called Sulla made himself dictator of Rome (though he was careful not to call himself King). After his death fighting broke out again. The civil war raged on throughout Italy. The Italian tribes turned on Rome, demanding full citizenship. The war was stopped for a time by Julius Caesar, who was a "popular", and not at all fond of the Senate. They felt the same way about him.

Julius Caesar discovered that a Roman army could be made to follow the man who inspired their loyalty and paid them best. He got his legions into tip-top shape by campaigning in Gaul (another province added to the Empire). Then he halted at the boundary of Italy, a little stream called the Rubicon, and threatened to march on Rome if the Senate didn't grant certain little requests he made. They refused, and Caesar crossed the Rubicon. Rome fell, and another Dictator reigned: Caesar.

Julius Caesar

A rumour spread that Caesar meant to set himself up as King of Rome. It may even have been true. Anyhow, the rumour got him murdered on the Ides of March (March 15th) 44 B.C., by a group of "No-King-in-Rome" Republicans, and the civil wars broke out all over again. In the end the Republicans, Brutus and Cassius, were defeated by Caesar's lieutenant, Mark Antony, and a rather weedy boy of eighteen, Caesar's great-nephew and adopted son. His name was Octavian and nobody took much notice of him. "The young man," said Cicero,* "must be flattered, used, and pushed aside."

But if there was any using and pushing aside to be done, it was Octavian who did

* A famous lawyer, politician, and speech-maker. We still have a lot of his letters and speeches. He dithered badly in the Civil War, changing sides twice. He thought the pen was mightier than the sword. But Mark Antony, stung by his attacks, had Cicero's head cut off.

Cicero

it. Despite his youth and ill-health he turned out as tough and crafty as any veteran. He leant on Antony during the crisis, waited till the old soldier became friendly with Cleopatra, and then, using his cold sense of timing, knocked them both for six at the sea-battle of Actium, in

September 31 B.C. This left him in command of the whole Roman world. Rome had at last met its match: the Civil Wars

Octavian

were over. So, though no one knew it till long afterwards, was the Roman Republic.

Octavian was determined not to make the same mistakes that Sulla and Caesar had done. One principle guided him. He must hold supreme power, but must always *appear* to be a mere "First Citizen". He flattered the Senate. He put senators in control of unimportant provinces. He kept up the elaborate pretence that Rome was still a Republic. But of course it was not; it had become a real Empire, and Octavian was its first Emperor. The Senate voted him the title of "Augustus", which means "worthy of honour", and it is as Augustus that we know him today. He was a clever man, but a very cold one. He had to be.

Coin showing the head of the Emperor Tiberius

Who was to succeed him after his death? Augustus wanted a blood-relative, but was doomed to one disappointment after another. His various candidates all died— or were murdered. In the end he fell back on his wife's son by her first husband, Tiberius. The whole early history of the Empire is marked by crises over the succession. Blood-relatives were all very well, but the family tree tended to throw up dangerous lunatics like Caligula and Nero. On the other hand, how else was a new Emperor to be chosen?

After Nero's death (he was the last of the line) a year's civil war produced four Emperors in quick succession. The army, as a Roman historian said, had found out that Emperors could be made outside Rome, and there were plenty of commanders—in Germany, or Palestine—who fancied their chances. For a while a system

of adoption was used: this produced the great philosopher-Emperor Marcus Aurelius. But *he* chose his own son, a tough man called Commodus who fancied himself as a gladiator. Chaos returned again.

So the unwieldy Empire went on its way, affected less by changes of Emperor than you might think. Constantine (A.D. 306–337) made Christianity the official religion. A second capital was established in the East, at Constantinople,

Commodus as Hercules

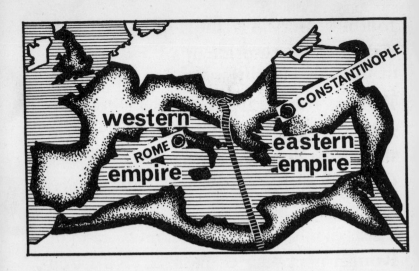

and survived to rule over what was left of the Empire after Rome fell. This is what we mean when we talk about the "Byzantine Empire". By now everyone in the Empire was technically a Roman citizen, though he might be anything by birth from a Spaniard to a Thracian. (There were even Spanish and Thracian Emperors, too.) The idea of true-blue Romans and Italians holding out against yelling barbarians is all wrong. By the fourth century A.D. most of the Roman Army itself was made up of barbarians.

Still, A.D. 476 does mark the end of Roman rule, and Augustulus Romulus *was* the last Western Emperor, even though he was a usurper. After that the Germanic tribes moved in; Vandals, and Goths, and Visigoths, and Ostrogoths. They didn't believe in Roman law or Roman plumbing or Roman civilization generally. *That* is what we mean by the end of the Roman Empire. It took nearly fifteen hundred years to get back central heating, decent sanitation, and well-planned private houses, not to mention roads worth the name and common-sense town-planning. Barbarians have never cared for such things.

But they couldn't stamp them out, either. About a third of our language is Latin still, and our laws are still based on

Roman Bridge at Nimes

those the Romans made. Architects copy their bridges and public buildings. The men who ran British India imitated their provincial administration. They are the most modern people in many ways till our own time. That is why they are so fascinating to read about.

2

The Roman People

IN OLD bound volumes of *Punch* you
may have found cartoons about a char-
acter called Sir Gorgius Midas. He is fat,
vulgar, and absolutely dripping with
money. He drops aitches right left and
centre. He has made his fortune from
nothing, and is going to let everyone know
it. In ways the Romans were rather like
Sir Gorgius. They began as a group of
small, thrifty peasant-farmers, and never
quite got over having an Empire to run.

LR–C

The peasant streak kept coming out in them when they were the richest nation in the known world.

They were coarse, shrewd, practical, and somewhat unimaginative. They had no great authors or artists at the time of the Punic Wars. But they felt that anyone going to the top *must* have poets and philosophers and suchlike, (a) because it meant they were a pretty crude lot if they hadn't, and (b) to write stuff saying what jolly good chaps were running the Roman government. Nowadays we call this propaganda. They didn't have a name for it in Rome, but it came to the same thing.

So they looked around, and found that the Greeks had just what they wanted; art, literature, everything. They borrowed and copied it all as fast as they could. They took over Greek myths because the Roman ones were so dim and peasantish. They had

Greek slave-teachers and slave-accountants and slave-doctors and slave-poets. These clever foreigners were useful, but also made their Roman masters feel terribly inferior. This is probably why the Romans went on and on about how nasty and tricksy and over-clever the Greeks were, not straightforward chaps you could trust at all, oh no.

The Romans were very self-conscious about having been peasants. That is why they treated their slaves so badly, worse than the Greeks had ever done. (One Roman handbook on farming recommends you to get rid of old harness and worn-out slaves in the same breath.) They felt so unsure of themselves that they had to take it out on those under them. Besides, they had hundreds and hundreds of cheap slaves. After the Punic Wars and the capture of countries like Spain, prisoners-of-war came streaming in. They were all sold in the slave-markets.

Originally, of course, the Romans had lived very little better than slaves themselves. They worked long, back-breaking hours on the land. Their wives and daughters stayed at home to spin and weave and cook. The head of the household had absolute authority: he could even put his sons to death. These early Romans believed in being thrifty, sober, hard-working, serious-minded, unambitious. If there was a war they all went off from the fields and fought, and then went back again afterwards without a murmur.

But when they suddenly found themselves immensely rich and powerful, it went to their peasant heads. Up till now they hadn't had much to do with more civilized countries abroad. But after the Punic Wars even the most upright Roman could see that the good time was going on somewhere else, and why shouldn't the victorious nation get a slice of the cake? Rich exotic food, gold plate, silk dresses, Greek statues, a whole gorgeous beanfeast was theirs for the taking. Shiploads of loot docked at Ostia, the port of Rome: rare jewellery and glassware, pictures, luxuries of all sorts. The Romans had never had it so good, and they overdid things as a result.

They went in for enormous banquets, and got ill. They became very dishonest. The more they had, the more they wanted. Sons pranced about in Greek tunics, and answered their fathers back when told to stop it. Wives and daughters decked themselves out in silks and ear-rings and left the weaving and spinning to slave-girls. The divorce-rate rocketed, and nobody cared. Politicians were bribed wholesale. More and more of the real work was done by slaves. Money, lots of it, was everyone's first object in life. Some, especially in Rome, got it. Others, the vast majority, didn't.

Of course, it's easy to exaggerate all this. Things must have worked efficiently enough—in fact we know they did—for the Empire to have lasted close on five hundred years. Lots of people were sober, honest, devoted to their wives, and not particularly greedy. But when you look at a town like Pompeii, which was a sort of seaside resort for rich businessmen, you can see what wealth did to the Romans.

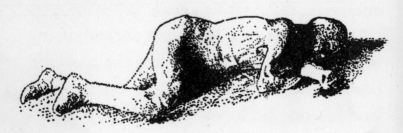

Plaster cast made from a corpse in devastated Pompeii

Pompeii is a stupendously vulgar place. The people who lived there worshipped money, and had the most appalling taste in art. Most of the wealthy residents— fish-sauce kings and the like—smothered their walls with bad copies of late Greek paintings. Their big houses were stuffed with furniture and bronzes and smart expensive knick-knacks. But they had pleasant gardens, with pools and fountains, and the central hall of the house, the *atrium*, was open to the sky. The rain drained down from a square sky-light into a shallow marble basin. Summer in Italy is very hot, so there were lots of cool verandahs and colonnades.

Some people, especially in Rome, lived in tall blocks of flats very like the modern ones you can see there today. These were badly built, and were always falling down or catching fire. Fire was the big danger in a crowded city like Rome, even though the water supply then was actually bigger than it is now—the aqueducts saw to that. But there was no proper fire brigade, and, more important, no hydraulic hoses. The Greeks and Romans knew about hydraulics, but only used such things for temple miracles. Why invent machines when you had plenty of slaves handy?

Outside the cities life in Italy was very much the same under the Roman Empire as it is now. The railway is the only big difference. Travel through Calabria or the Abruzzi hill-country today, and you will still see peasant-farmers living and working as they did two thousand years ago— ploughing with oxen, tending their vines and olives, scraping a bare living from the soil. Many villages are without electricity, and you will find oil-lamps in use not so very different from those of the ancient

Romans. Everyone then, rich and poor alike, got up early to catch the first light, and went to bed soon after it was dark.

But this was about the only thing rich and poor had in common. The division between them was enormous, far bigger than anything we see today. The rich were stupendously rich, multi-millionaires, and there were only a few thousand of them. These are the people, by and large, that you read about in the history books. Some of them were not only rich but aristocratic as well, and they were the people who filled the Senate, fought the wars, and ran the country. From time to time a poor plebeian managed to reach the top, but this tended to have disastrous results. The peasant-general Marius was Consul seven times, and was savagely attacked for ignorant brutality by the aristocratic historians.

The non-aristocratic millionaires were most of them *equites*. We translate this word "knights", but it really means "horsemen". At the beginning of Rome's history the *equites* were citizens who could afford a horse and armour in time of war. Later this was changed to a cash payment, and the "knights" were simply business-men who had more than a certain fixed income. Later still, even ex-slaves and foreigners became successful speculators. We have a picture of one such slave-millionaire, Trimalchio, in a book written during Nero's reign by a dandy called Petronius.

It was the people at the top who had the rare banquets and orgies, and did the things we think about when the Romans are mentioned, like invading Gaul and build-ing bridges and defending Hadrian's Wall. But they are not the people you would have brushed shoulders with in a crowded street if you were transported back to Rome in Augustus's time: any more than you are likely to meet a Cabinet Minister or a multi-millionaire walking round London. Rome and Italy were populated with millions of people, slaves and free men, who lived very near the bread-line and whose hard work made the million-aires' paradise possible.

There were surveyors and architects and market officials, tax-collectors, lawyers' clerks and notaries, scribes and draughts-men, shop-keepers, coppersmiths, builders, armourers, water-carriers, school-teachers, bath-attendants, bakers, poulterers—the list could go on for ever. It includes a lot of jobs that today are done by machines. These faceless workers from the past seldom get in the history-books unless they are in rebellion. But from buried towns like Pompeii we can learn how important they were—and how like our-selves. They fell in love, scribbled on walls, couldn't spell, grumbled at taxes, rooted for their local gladiator or election candidate. They remind us that the Romans were real people, not just stage-figures swathed in togas.

So when we say "the Romans" we mean a lot of things. By the end of the Roman Empire we mean not only the people in Rome itself, rich and poor, slave or free; not even all those in the municipalities of Italy; but every citizen whatsoever. He might be a Spaniard or a Briton, a North African Berber or a Syrian, but he still acknowledged Roman law, claimed Roman privileges, and probably spoke at least a recognizable sort of pidgin-Latin. As a Roman citizen he could travel without let or hindrance throughout the length and breadth of Mediterranean Europe. Can we say as much today?

3

Public Life

ROMAN government is puzzling but rather fun. Romans were always very good at saying one thing and in fact doing another, especially when power was involved. You remember how Augustus became an absolute ruler but pretended the Senate was ruling with him, and the Republic was still going strong? Well, that wasn't anything new: the dodge had worked very well under the Republic too. Only then it was the Senate that ran

*Ruins of Aqueduct
at Rome*

everything, and made it look as though the people were in control. To an outside observer the whole thing might seem democratic; but it wasn't.

The Romans were very conservative people. They disliked change, and had a healthy respect for blue blood. They felt in their bones that it was better for a small group of aristocrats to be running things. The voters were allowed to hold assemblies and make laws, up to a point. But the real power belonged to the Senate. Most senators were ex-magistrates. They formed a tight-knit little club, and fixed things the way they wanted, without any fuss. They were gentlemen all, and didn't like social gatecrashers, or "new men", as they called them. The great politician Cicero was in this unlucky class. His father was a "freedman"—that is, a slave who had bought his liberty.

Cicero's brother Quintus wrote an electioneering handbook for him. It contained these words: "Every day, when you go down to the Forum [Rome's big central square] to canvas for votes, say to yourself: *I am a new man; I am a candidate for the consulship; and this is Rome.*" So if you wanted to have a career in Roman government it was as well to start off with the right parents and background. Even then you had a long struggle ahead of you before you could reach the top of the ladder as Consul.

You got the vote when you were seventeen, but you couldn't hold *any* public office till you had done ten years' army service. If you were well-connected, your army rank was that of "military tribune". There is nothing quite like this in the British Army today. It was like being a company commander *and* a staff officer. Then, when you were twenty-seven, you could stand for the "quaestorship". Quaestors were financial officers, who looked after the Roman army's money, and the Treasury as well.

The order in which you tried for these jobs was strictly laid down. You couldn't skip any of them. What's more, there had to be a gap of two clear years between your holding one official post and the next. The successful quaestor could, if he wanted, go straight on and run for "praetor". The praetors were rather like High Court Judges. They didn't normally try cases themselves, but nominated juries and summed up the legal procedures for them. They spent their year of office in Rome, and the following year went out on circuit to the provinces. When they took up office they used to publish an edict, on special white boards, saying the maxims and principles of law they would follow during the year. (This was called an *album*, the Latin word for "white"— we still use it.)

But quite a few ambitious young men liked to hold the "aedileship" before they became praetor—especially if they had a lot of money to spend. This wasn't because they particularly wanted to supervise the police and the fire service (such as it was), or to dole out free corn to the poor, or control the public markets, all of which jobs fell to the aedile. No indeed. The great attraction about being aedile was that you were responsible for organizing the public games. The more money you spent on a lavish show, with lots of wild beasts and gladiators, the more people were likely to vote for you again next time.

And so, finally, if you were lucky, you were elected consul: the highest civic office Rome could bestow. The consuls (there were always two of them) acted as chief magistrates, looked after foreign affairs, conducted elections. From 146 B.C. onwards they gradually ceased to lead the army—though lots of ex-consuls got high military commands after their year of office. But the honour and prestige of the consulship were tremendous, and men still angled for it under the Empire, when the consuls had no real power at all. Far more powerful Imperial posts were those of the Prefect of Egypt, who controlled Rome's corn-supply, and the two Praetorian Prefects,

who commanded the troops stationed in Rome. Later they extended their authority over all the armies in Italy. There were two of them as a safety precaution, in case one turned traitor. Sometimes they both did. This caused no end of trouble.

But for most people such plums remained far out of reach. Full Roman citizenship was the most they could hope for. This meant you had the right to vote (as your patron told you), hold office (if anyone would put you up), own property (if you could afford it) and contract a "legal" marriage. You could also "appeal to the people" if convicted of a crime. Freedmen—such as Cicero's father—had most of these rights, but couldn't run for public office. If you committed certain crimes—evading military service or taxation, for instance—you could lose your citizenship.

4

Private Life and Pastimes

PEOPLE in Rome lived out of doors much more than we do. This was partly because for much of the year Italy is a very hot country, and partly because the Italians were a naturally sociable people. They still are. You will find them, now as two thousand years ago, gathering in public squares and wine-shops, discussing politics with enormous excitement and gusto, using flowery language rather like Cicero's. Ancient Romans, like modern

Italians, adored making speeches, and saw no point in concealing their emotions. They exaggerated, swore at each other, and lost their tempers at regular intervals. It was all enormous fun, especially for the people at the top. They could make speeches in the Forum or the law-courts without anyone daring to answer back.

Let's look at the daily routine of an average wealthy Roman. His lighting was no better than anyone else's, so he would be early to bed (unless he'd been drinking) and up at crack of dawn. For a rich man he was very primitive in ways. He slept in his underwear, and soap didn't mean much to him. His breakfast was a glass of water. He dressed in a loin-cloth and a tunic. By the time of Augustus the heavy draped toga was going out of fashion. It was cumbersome to put on and soon wore out. People preferred a Greek-style cloak.

A rich Roman never really *worked* at all; the nearest he got to it was being a landlord or a shareholder in a big company. His first call of the day was to the barber's. He might not wash much before breakfast, but he took his hair and beard seriously. Then he would receive his "clients". These weren't clients in our sense of the word, but paid hangers-on who voted the way he told them, and did little jobs for him. Meanwhile his wife would be just as busy, with a squad of slave-girls dressing her, curling her hair, putting on her make-up, manicuring her, and generally preparing her for the day ahead. She didn't wash much, though, either.

For the rest of the morning your rich Roman might spend his time down in the Forum—a big public square where everything went on from political speeches to

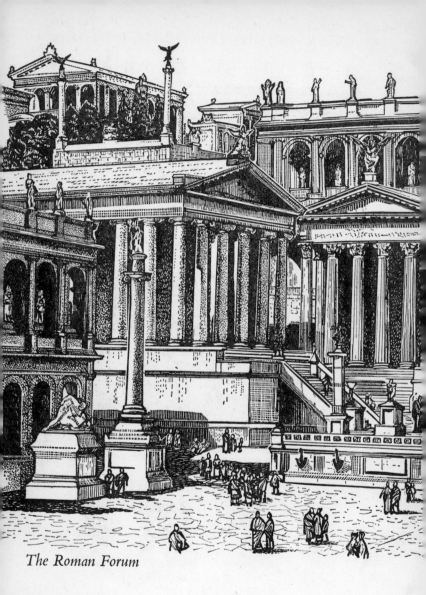

The Roman Forum

court cases and big business (See the picture on pages 58-9). It was a sort of cross between the Stock Exchange, Smithfield Market, and Hyde Park Corner. It was quite likely that he would have a legal case on hand himself. The Romans were fond of suing each other. The only professions a gentleman could follow were politics or the law. In neither case could he accept fees—not officially, that is.

Another attraction was the public reading. Rome had no cinemas, television, radio, or newspapers, and not much in the way of a theatre. So writers declaiming their own new works could pull in a good audience, though there were so many of them that their hoarse bawling deafened the passers-by at times. A lot of these readings, though, were private, organized by rich patrons in their town or country houses.

After lunch—most often a light snack—the real fun of the day began, for rich and poor alike. In terms of cash the needy Roman did badly. But in working hours and subsidies he was better off than any working-class man till the days of trade unions. (He had unions of a sort, too.) He worked a maximum eight-hour day, which was chopped down to six, seven, or even fewer hours during the summer. There were innumerable public holidays—159 at one point—when he didn't work at all. Thousands of people drew the corn-dole. The people who got the worst of it (they often do) were the "intellectuals"—writers, poets, philosophers and "rhetoricians", who were a sort of free-lance university don, ready to give anyone a higher education for quick cash.

Best of all, from everybody's point of view, were the lavish official entertain-

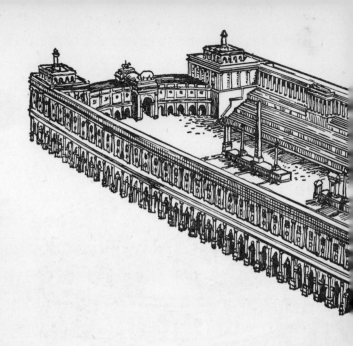

The Circus Maximus

ments provided throughout the year. You could go to the theatre or the Greek games, but this was reckoned pretty tame, sissy stuff. The two big attractions were the chariot races and the gladiatorial shows. The races were held in the Circus

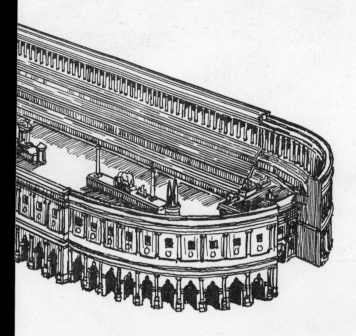

Maximus, a vast stadium 600 × 200 yards in size. Each race was seven laps, totalling nearly three miles. Tactics were very dirty· A good charioteer was as famous as a top racing driver today, and made masses of money; but he didn't often last long.

Enormous bets were laid on the favourites.

The gladiatorial shows have got the Romans a worse name than anything else, and rightly so. You can't get round it, they thoroughly *enjoyed* seeing people ripped up by wild beasts, or fighting each other to the death. That was what the Colosseum was built for; and the Colosseum (besides being colossal) was meant to last. It could seat at least 50,000 spectators. The arena was 50 yards wide and over 80 long, and could be flooded for mock naval battles. In this arena tigers, lions, leopards, elephants and other animals were shot down—5,000 died in one day during the Games of the Emperor Titus in A.D. 80. Human blood was spilt just as recklessly. One monster show in A.D. 113 lasted 117 days, and 4,941 pairs of gladiators took part in it. Criminals were thrown to wild beasts unarmed; these "criminals" included many Christian martyrs.

Protests were few and feeble. The Romans frankly enjoyed torture and blood-letting. They were tough, brutal peasants still, peasants on the grand scale,

LR—E

peasants with ample money but little imagination. Whatever their gifts to us, they were in ways absolutely disgusting people, and we should never forget it.

After the afternoon's entertainment most Romans would pay a visit to the public baths. If they failed to wash in the morning, they made up for it now. These baths were more like Turkish baths than the sort we have today. When you had undressed you went into the "warm room". Next door was the "cold room", where you took a plunge. From here you moved on to the "hot room" and lastly to the "sweating room", which was so roasting that you perspired all over. The steam-heat was piped under the floors and up the walls by a system of central heating. You can see one of these baths in England—at Bath, which the Romans called Aquae Sulis.

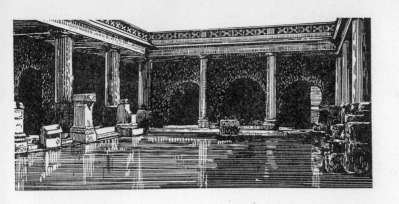

These baths were not just places where you washed; they formed a kind of club too. There were shops and gardens on the premises, gymnasiums, massage-rooms, sometimes even libraries. Women could use them as well as men, but not (under the Empire, anyway) at the same time. If you still felt energetic you could wrestle or play ball-games there. But by the time you were through the sun would be low; it was time to think about dinner.

The Romans certainly did themselves well at their evening meal. But we should remember (a) that they ate practically nothing else during the day, and (b) that the real gluttonous orgies we read about were the exception rather than the rule. Dinner was a formal occasion. You ate in a special dining-room, on couches. There were always three couches, set round a square table in the middle. Where you sat (or reclined) was fixed by your social status. The couch opposite the empty side of the table was the highest.

You had knives and spoons, but not forks, so you ate with your fingers, and cleaned up between courses. If you fancied any tit-bits you hadn't room for you could take them away afterwards in your table-napkin. An elaborate dinner would start with *hors d'oeuvre* — egg mayonnaise, cucumbers, mussels, oysters, vegetables and, yes, *dormice*. Next came the roast, with meat and poultry. Afterwards, fruit and sweets. The huge menus we read about were the equivalent of a Lord Mayor's Banquet, something quite out of the ordinary. Most people were less ambitious. When the poet Martial asked a friend round he promised him an *hors d'oeuvre* of haggis, eggs, fish, herbs and lettuce; ham, sausages, chicken and broiled kid to follow; with fruit for dessert. We still have a Roman cookery book, and its simple recipes suggest that when guests weren't expected dinner was very plain indeed.

5

Buildings, roads, aqueducts

WHATEVER the Romans were not, they were undoubtedly practical. Like the Colosseum, their roads, temples, gateways, baths, triumphal arches, their country houses and villas, even their aqueducts and sewers, were built to last. They were all for having things comfortable and efficient. They slashed their roads straight ahead, through hillsides and over valleys, for the legions to move quickly anywhere, and to make it easy for Rome

to keep in touch with the provinces.
These roads were better than anything
till our own macadamized surfaces. First
the earth was rammed flat. Then came a
layer of hand-sized stones. On this was
laid a nine-inch layer of rubble and lime,

topped with concrete. Above came the paving, of blocks or flint. The main roads were well drained, and equipped with milestones. They criss-crossed the whole Empire. There are 5,000 known miles of Roman roads in Britain, for the most part still used.

Italy was a good country for building in stone. Its quarries turned out endless hard travertine and marble. The Romans built huge defensive walls and towers and gates. The early ones didn't look pretty, but they were solid and kept enemies out, which was what they were meant to do. Since Rome grew up on both sides of a wide river, the Tiber, the Romans learnt a lot about bridge-building, too. They sank their foundations so firmly that many of these triple-arched stone bridges are still in use today: you can find them all over Europe.

MAIN ROMAN ROADS

Roman temples are like Greek temples, only more so. They are large, heavy, over-decorated, with too many columns. The Romans could turn anything into a kind of municipal town-hall when they copied it. If you ever have the luck to stand in the excavated Forum at Rome you'll see what I mean. No one ever touched the Romans for civic monstrosities. Their public statues are lumpish and pompous, their public buildings vulgar on the grand scale. A large number of local authorities in Great Britain still go on copying both. This is a pity, and don't let anyone tell you the opposite.

What the Romans did really well were roads and bridges, triumphal arches and public baths. Here they had a practical end in view and knew what they were at. Their amphitheatres (this is what they called gladiatorial arenas) are first-rate, too, for obvious reasons. Some Emperors, like Nero, went in for strange buildings that we call follies. Nero's Golden House spread over most of the Palatine Hill in Rome, and must have been a first-class eyesore. On the other hand the Romans also built beautiful country farmhouses, like the one at Chedworth in Gloucestershire. Agriculture, and the life that went with it, was something they understood.

But it was their curious passion for water

that produced the engineering works we still best remember them by—their aqueducts and sewers. There are no less than eleven main aqueducts converging on Rome. They cost the earth, supplied the city with an unbelievable amount of water, and are fantastic engineering achievements. One of them, the Aqua Claudia, has a continuous three-mile stretch of tunnel. At Segovia in Spain there is a double-tiered aqueduct bridge some 800 yards long, with 109 arches.

All this water had to have an outlet as well; and the result was the best system of sewage and draining in the whole of the ancient world. The Greeks never bothered much about drains. But the Etruscans did, and the Romans took the hint. The biggest sewer was called the Cloaca Maxima, which means just that: the biggest sewer. It was vaulted and paved like a railway

tunnel, and it is still in use. A friend of Augustus, the great general Agrippa, actually rowed up it from its outfall in the Tiber. The water-level in Rome today has risen about nine feet, so you couldn't do the same—even supposing you wanted to.

6

The Roman Army

IN THE early days of the Republic the Roman army was a pretty makeshift affair. Professional soldiers, a "regular army" as we understand it, simply didn't exist. Citizens were called up "for the duration", and went back to their farms when the campaign was over. What sort of soldier you were was decided by your income—like so many things at Rome. The richest served in the cavalry. Those not quite so wealthy (but still pretty well off) formed the heavy-armed infantry. There were four lower classes, each with progressively less equipment. In a real crisis the poorest citizens would be called up and provided with arms by the State. If you were under seventeen or over forty-six you were only liable for garrison duty.

This system worked well enough while Rome was still a small city-state. But after the Punic Wars (which went on a very long time) things had to be changed. A citizen army wouldn't do. For one thing, a campaign lasting more than one season ruined the crops: all the farm-hands were away fighting. For another, you couldn't raise enough men that way. So Marius, the peasant-general, threw the army open to everyone, whether they had any property or not. The pay wasn't high, but it attracted a lot of out-of-work adventurers.

The basic army unit was the legion. Its

A Roman Standard

official strength was about 6,000 men. From Marius's time the legionary was armed with a short javelin, the *pilum,* which he threw at the enemy before the hand-to-hand sword-fighting began. He also had a shield, a helmet, and a reinforced leather cuirass. The usual battle order consisted of three lines. The legion was divided into ten cohorts, or companies. Four of these fought in the front line, three each in the two rear ranks. Julius Caesar gave the legions official numbers and eagle standards. This meant that each of them had its own tradition, like a British regiment—such as the famous Twentieth Legion, the Valeria Victrix, stationed

80

A Roman Legionary

LR-F

for several centuries in this country.

After the Civil Wars at the end of the Republic there were about fifty legions. Most of the legionaries during these campaigns signed on with an individual commander, for as long as his command lasted. Augustus changed all this. He established a permanent army much as we know it. Legionaries could sign on for twenty years, with the prospect of a bonus and land when they retired. Enlistment carried full citizenship with it. Augustus reduced the legions to eighteen at first; there were twenty-five after his death. Later this figure rose to just over thirty.

A legion was commanded by a Legate, more or less the same as a modern divisional general. Under him were six company officers, the military tribunes, and a camp quartermaster. Each cohort was controlled by a centurion, a long-term soldier who was sergeant-major and subaltern rolled into one. Every legion had a squadron of cavalry allotted to it. The crack troops of the Praetorian Guard served only sixteen years instead of twenty and got three times the ordinary rate of pay—mostly to prevent revolutions.

This was the sort of army with which Caesar attacked this country in 55 B.C., and which stayed here—after the final invasion of A.D. 43—as a permanent garrison. Caesar felt Britain *had* to be conquered. It was a handy refuge across the Channel for every sort of rebel. British Druids preached nationalism and insurrection—they were behind the famous revolt of Boadicea. The Roman peace must be kept at all costs. Caesar, alas, made rather a nonsense of the invasion. He underestimated the Channel gales, which carved up his fleet. Reinforcements mutinied.

Supplies were uncertain. But Caesar won a battle and got at least one big chief to submit. After that he quickly returned to Gaul.

From then on the Romans got the idea of invading Britain stuck in their minds as something that must be done because Caesar said so. Caligula, the mad Emperor, set his soldiers picking up shells on the beach. It was left to the elderly Claudius to finish off the job properly. London and Colchester formed early Roman centres, and from here the Romans fanned out north and west, to Wroxeter, Silchester, and Lincoln. The roads they built—like Watling Street to Wroxeter—were first laid down for troops and supplies.

But the resistance movement against Rome took a long time to stamp out. One British leader, Caractacus, became a sort

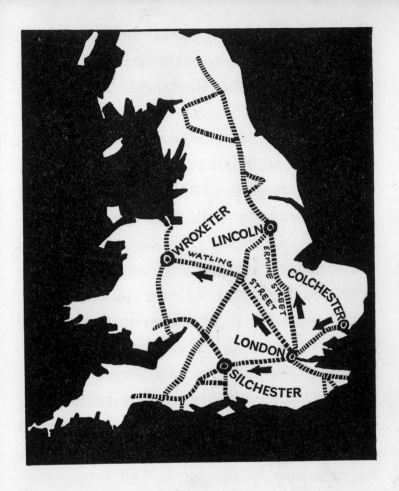

of guerrilla general, raiding the Romans from the Welsh hills. He held out for nearly ten years, till the Roman commander Ostorius smashed him in open battle, taking his wife and daughter prisoner. Caractacus escaped, but a pro-Roman British Queen, Cartimandua, sent him back to Ostorius in chains. He spent the rest of his life a captive at Rome. He was the son of Cymbeline, and some people think he was the original King Arthur.

The story of Boadicea is far more horrible. She was Queen of the Iceni tribe, who lived in what is now East Anglia. Her husband, King Prasutagus, had surrendered to Claudius without fighting, and was allowed to reign as a "client" king—that is, a puppet of Rome. But when Prasutagus died, the Romans tightened up on the Iceni. The Emperor's "procurator", or financial agent, confiscated royal property and raided the palace. Boadicea was flogged, and her daughters attacked. Members of the Iceni nobility were seized as slaves. The Romans pressed harshly for more tribute, more recruits.

The tribesmen responded to Boadicea's call. The Governor, Suetonius Paulinus, was far away in North Wales. Boadicea and her followers sacked Colchester, and smashed the Ninth Legion that marched to intercept them from Lincoln. Suetonius Paulinus was forced to let Boadicea storm through both London and Verulamium (St. Albans) unopposed. She had her vengeance there indeed. No prisoners were taken, no quarter given. Deep down under London, archaeologists everywhere come to the layer of ashes and bones that marks the furious Queen's passing. In the two towns, it is said, 70,000 people perished.

Suetonius Paulinus caught Boadicea in open country and, with magnificent gene-

Boadicea

ralship, annihilated her forces. Boadicea committed suicide. Suetonius began a reign of terror, with widespread police posts and endless "punitive expeditions". He thought kindness to the natives was mere weakness. But even in Rome, enough was enough. A ravaged province could not produce its quota of tribute and goods.

So Nero recalled Suetonius, and a new procurator was sent out to patch up the quarrels and conciliate the rebels. His name was Julius Classicianus, and he deserves to be remembered. At least he gave war-torn Britain peace—even though it was mainly for the sake of the Roman Treasury.

7

Decline and fall

SOON enough, though, Britain grew used to having the Romans in occupation. Roman roads ran in a network across the countryside, ignoring the old grass tracks such as the Icknield Way. Roman traders brought ready cash for British hides and dyes. British nobles married legionaries' daughters, adopted Roman dress and habits, built steam-baths and open-air theatres and country villas. A new way of life came into being—not

Roman, not British, but "Romano-British". Yet when at last Rome collapsed, and the legions left Britain, that way of life vanished as though it had never been. Only the ruins we find here and there—at St. Alban's or Bath or the Scottish frontier, where the Emperor Hadrian built his great Wall against the raiding Picts—remind us that Britain was once a Roman province, with a centuries-old tradition of Roman life.

What was happening in Rome all this time? What do we mean when we talk about Rome's "decline and fall"? The picture of a sort of civilized sandcastle, crumbling before waves of barbarians, is hopelessly misleading. It is true that German tribesmen hammered away at the frontiers harder and harder as time went on. But the real problem lay in the Roman Empire itself. All the time it had been changing, without people realizing the fact. More and more foreigners got the citizenship. After Constantine's reign the old Gods were abandoned in favour of Christianity. Having two capitals, one in Rome and the other at Constantinople, weakened the idea of an indivisible Empire. Perhaps people just got tired of efficiency and civilization. When the Roman legions left Britain, the incoming Saxons never, as far as we know, took over a Roman villa. Such luxury was not for them.

The crumbling walls tell their own story. The villagers at the mouth of the Tiber saw their small wattled town grow till it was a marble city ruling the whole of the Mediterranean. Roman roads and Roman ships carried traders and civil servants and soldiers to country after country, stamping it with the pattern of a Roman province,

As colonists the Romans were excellent—so long as people wanted to be colonized. It is an old story, and we can see it happening again today. In the end Roman civilization became tired and old. "Rome" no longer meant enough to the men who manned the frontiers, who were not Roman by blood. When the barbarians finally took over control of the Empire, it was mainly barbarians they defeated.

That is why we talk, today, of the "Golden Age" of Rome, the time when the idea of the Empire was new and exciting, and sparked soldiers and statesmen and writers to great achievements. The "Golden Age" is a short one: perhaps a century before and after Augustus. But this was when everything that makes Rome worth remembering happened—the great poets like Virgil and Horace, the finest building, the most original ideas.

This is the Rome that still lives on in later civilizations. It will always be worth exploring, and always have something new to tell us. It is proof against all barbarians, even today.

33/30